D0824729

How Many Weeks?

by Katherine Krieg

Say Hello to Amicus Readers.

You'll find our helpful dog, Amicus, chasing a ball—to let you know the reading level of a book.

① ② ③

Learn to Read

Frequent repetition, high frequency words, and close photo-text matches introduce familiar topics and provide ample support for brand new readers.

Read Independently

Some repetition is mixed with varied sentence structures and a select amount of new vocabulary words are introduced with text and photo support.

Read to Know More

Interesting facts and engaging art and photos give fluent readers fun books both for reading practice and to learn about new topics.

Amicus Readers are published by Amicus
P.O. Box 1329, Mankato, MN 56002
www.amicuspublishing.us

Photo Credits: Stephanie Frey/Shutterstock Images, cover; Ksenia Ragozina/Shutterstock Images, 1; Shutterstock Images, 3, 6–7, 8–9, 16; iStock/Thinkstock, 5, 14–15; Rob Hainer/Shutterstock Images, 10; iStockphoto, 13

Produced for Amicus by The Peterson Publishing Company and Red Line Editorial.

Editor Jenna Gleisner
Designer Becky Daum

Library of Congress
Cataloging-in-Publication Data
Krieg, Katherine, author.
  How many weeks? / by Katherine Krieg.
    pages cm. -- (Amicus readers level 2) (Measuring time)
  Summary: "Introduces activities young readers experience in a matter of weeks, such as attending summer camp, while teaching ways to measure a week and how it compares to days and months."-- Provided by publisher.
  Audience: K to grade 3
  ISBN 978-1-60753-724-3 (library binding)
  ISBN 978-1-60753-828-8 (ebook)
  1. Time--Juvenile literature. 2. Time measurements--Juvenile literature. I. Title.
  QB209.5.K757 2014
  529.7--dc23
                                      2014049948

Printed in Malaysia
10 9 8 7 6 5 4 3 2 1

We use weeks to measure time. One week is 7 days. What can you do in 1 week during the summer?

Logan will spend

1 week

at summer camp. His dad
shows him on a calendar.
A week is 1 whole row.

August

SUNDAY	MONDAY	TUESDAY	WEDNESDAY	THURSDAY	FRIDAY	SATURDAY
					1	2
3	4	5	6	7	8	9
10	11	12	13	14	15	16
17	18	19	20	21	22	23
24 / 31	25	26	27	28	29	30

1 week

At camp, James sees a caterpillar. In about 7 to 10 days it will make a chrysalis to become a butterfly.

Ten days is

1 and a half weeks.

Rae waits for the seed she planted to grow. She marks off days on a calendar. She sees a sprout after 14 days. That is **2 weeks.**

Aria is learning to swim at camp. She can swim across the entire pool after practicing for 3 weeks.

Luke lost a tooth this summer.
It will take about

4 weeks

for a new tooth to grow in.
That is 4 rows on a
calendar, or about

1 month!

So many things can
happen in 1 week.
**What can you
do in a week?**

Measuring Weeks

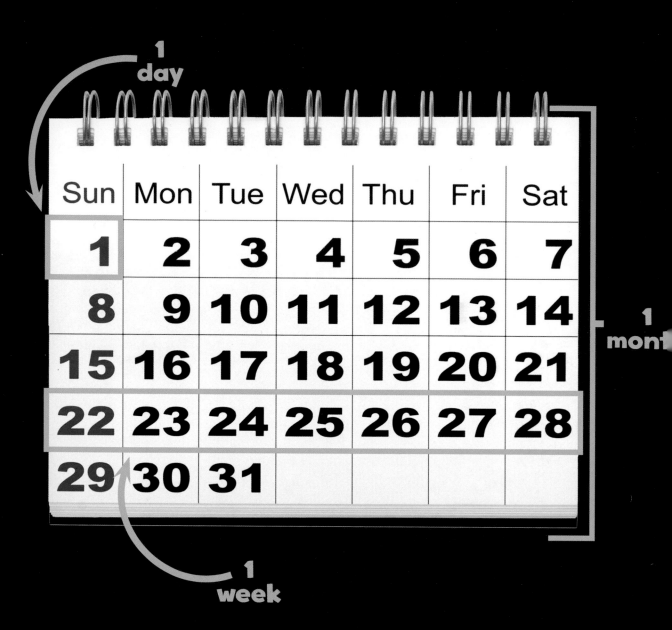

Sun	Mon	Tue	Wed	Thu	Fri	Sat
1	2	3	4	5	6	7
8	9	10	11	12	13	14
15	16	17	18	19	20	21
22	23	24	25	26	27	28
29	30	31				

1 day

1 month

1 week